HIGHLIGHTS *from* WELSH HISTORY
OPENING SOME WINDOWS ON OUR PAST

EMRYS ROBERTS

First impression: 2017
© Emrys Roberts & Y Lolfa Cyf., 2017

Cover design: Olwen Fowler

ISBN: 978 1 78461 389 1

Published and printed in Wales
on paper from well-maintained forests by
Y Lolfa Cyf., Talybont, Ceredigion SY24 5HE
e-mail ylolfa@ylolfa.com
website www.ylolfa.com
tel 01970 832 304
fax 832 782

Preface

For starters... let me ask you a few questions.

If I were to talk of a country that produced one of Europe's leading mathematical thinkers and one of the scientists who made the World Wide Web possible; a country that produced one of the Western world's most penetrative political thinkers, who influenced the direction taken by the new United States of America in the eighteenth century and whose death triggered a day of official mourning in France; a country that produced a pioneer of co-operation and one of the main instigators of the League of Nations, forerunner of the United Nations – could you name that country?

If I were to ask which nation boasted the most advanced laws in the Middle Ages; which produced Britain's only effective royal dynasty and its most effective prime minister; a country that produced a man probably more responsible than Charles Darwin for developing the theory of evolution and a woman at least as responsible as Florence Nightingale for developing the nursing profession – would you know which country I had in mind?

If I were to add that this country was the world leader during the early Industrial Revolution; a country that contained the world's first industrial town; that was home to the world's first steam train and the country where the red flag of revolution was first flown – would you be getting warmer?

If I added that it boasts a language and a literature twice as old as that of England's; that a poem about its bards is compulsory reading in all schools in Hungary; that its laws recognised women's rights a thousand years before England followed suit; that in proportion to its population it produces more professional opera singers than Italy; that an education system it pioneered inspired educational developments in Russia and in Cuba and that it produced the prototype modern guerrilla fighter – would you realise then that I am talking about Wales?

And that's just for starters! If you would like to know more about the huge contribution this small nation of Wales has made to the world – largely unknown because the world, and often we ourselves, view Wales through the mostly ignorant yet patronising eyes of the English – then read on.

Contents

Introduction

Not another book on Welsh history! Well yes, but read on and you'll find out why.

As the sub-title of the book suggests, I hope to open a few windows on Wales for people who may not know a great deal about our past. I've used the word 'window' for two reasons. Firstly, I have not tried to write a comprehensive, academic history. If that's what you are looking for, you should read the late John Davies's *A History of Wales*. Nor have I tried to write a concise continuous history of our country, like that of Gerald Morgan. In spite of books such as these, however, it appears that few Welsh people know much about the country in which they live. Many have little concept of what it means to be Welsh, other than cheering on the red jerseys rather than the white ones on the sports field.

This book is an attempt to throw some light on what appears to me to be significant periods and aspects of our past which have helped to make us what we are – brief glimpses rather than an in-depth study, but hopefully telling glimpses of the development of our nation.

Many years ago a respected history professor said to me: 'Roberts, your trouble is you try to understand history: all we want are the facts.' What an idiot,

I thought! There is little point in learning a series of historical facts by rote like a multiplication table. History must be based on facts of course, but grasping the bigger picture and understanding how we came to be what we are, are far more important. History is a bit like an Impressionist painting. The minute aspects of the painting are not vitally important; we need to stand back and take in the picture as a whole to appreciate its real impact.

My second reason for choosing the word 'windows' is because it is an Anglo-Saxon word related to Old German and Norse. This reminds us that much of what little is taught about Wales to children in school (if anything at all!) has not been from a Welsh perspective but rather from our neighbours' point of view. I cannot imagine the English being satisfied with a history of their country written, say, from a French point of view – or the French accepting a history of their country written by the English or the Germans!

The very words 'Wales' and 'Welsh' originate from Anglo-Saxon, meaning foreign or foreigners. The intent to make us feel foreign in our own land may have largely disappeared as official government policy, but that was certainly the original intention and, unfortunately, vestiges of it still remain today. If one reads the letters column of our newspapers, it would appear that some people think that Welsh speakers are a privileged minority – that all the best jobs are reserved for them! How is it then that so many of the top jobs in Wales are taken by people who are not only unable to speak Welsh but, in fact, are not Welsh at all, many of them appearing to have little interest in or empathy with our country? They may perhaps be the best people for those jobs, but their number certainly gives the lie to the argument that Welsh speakers enjoy positive discrimination in their favour. And, in terms of ordinary people, anyone trying to insist on our right to use our own language in our own country will soon find he or she is regarded at best as a nuisance and often as a troublemaker. 'Why can't you speak English?' they ask, assuming that no other language is really worth preserving!

The attitude of many English people is that the only difference between us and the English is that we have a funny accent and unpronounceable place names and that we like to think we're good at singing and playing rugby. They just can't understand why some of us want to speak our own language instead of theirs. In the same way, of course, when they think of the Scots they think of kilted bagpipe players eating haggis, and of the Irish as Guinness-swilling dancers and storytellers. Unfortunately, because they know so little of their own national stories, many Welsh, Scots and Irish can scarcely argue with them.

Even in some (many?) schools where the Welsh language is the medium of instruction, very little Welsh history is taught – which in my view is an utter scandal and something which would not be tolerated in any other country. Popular news and entertainment media pay scant attention to Wales. If we feature at all, there is little if any understanding of what being Welsh means.

I believe the Welsh language is an important integral part of our heritage. But an awareness of the way we developed as a nation is even more important. Without such awareness, non-Welsh-speaking Welsh people – let alone immigrants from elsewhere – may see little point in learning the language when they can get by in English. Some understanding of our national identity is essential if the Welsh language and Wales as a nation are to survive.

Inevitably, history often deals in generalisations – especially in a small volume such as this. And generalisations, of course, never tell the whole story. I am sure there are many, many Welsh people who can't sing in tune, who don't play rugby and are not interested in the game. However, that does not undermine the truth of the generalisation that, especially in comparison with other nations, Welsh people love to sing (and on the whole are pretty good at it!) and get excited about the game of rugby.

The glimpses of our history which I have tried to capture in this volume do not, of course, tell the whole story of Wales by any means, but I hope what I have written will be enough to show why we should be proud of our small nation. You may be surprised at how rich our heritage is!

When Wales Began

Celtic Origins

Wales is one of the oldest nations in Europe. Indeed, since the idea of nationhood – something more than a tribe or a clan – is largely a European concept, Wales is one of the oldest nations on earth.

People inhabited the land we now call Wales before us, of course. Before the Roman Empire the peoples of Europe were still largely nomadic, moving from place to place in search of better land or minerals. People came to Wales from the Iberian Peninsula along sea routes which commenced in the Mediterranean. Later, the Celts swept across much of Europe from the east and settled along Europe's western seaboard. They developed what was probably the first relatively sophisticated culture in Europe north of the Alps. Traces of the Celts – especially their ornate metalwork, but traces of their language too – can be found in many parts of Europe.

There is a tomb of a Celtic chieftain near Hallein in Austria (where, incidentally, an information sheet is available in Welsh as well as other languages). This is a salt producing area, with a fantastic salt mine reflected in the name Hallein and the lakeside town of Hallstadt – 'halen' being the Welsh word for salt. Salt was a very important commodity at the time as it helped to preserve food. Payment was sometimes made with salt – hence the word 'salary' and the saying someone is 'worth his or her salt'. The major river in the area, of course, is the Danube – Donau in German – probably originating from the same word as the Welsh for waves, 'tonnau'.

Over time the Celtic language divided into two distinct linguistic groups – those speaking Goidelic in Ireland, the Isle of Man and northern Scotland, and those speaking Brythonic in what is present-day England, southern Scotland, Wales and Cornwall. The Brythons, of course, are the people from whom the name Britain is derived. At this time it could be argued that a British nation was indeed developing throughout Wales and across much of England and lowland Scotland.

The Romans

But then, the Romans came – their first tentative foray some fifty years before Christ, with the invasion and colonisation of what are now England and Wales starting some hundred years later. The Romans were fiercely resisted for many years by the various Brythonic tribes under the leadership of chieftains like Caradog (Caractacus) and Buddug (Boudica), both of whom earned the respect of Rome for their bravery. Caradog is remembered for his defiant speech when hauled before his eventual captors in Rome. It seems our ancestors were great orators even then!

The Roman historian Tacitus described the Silures, who lived in what is now south-eastern Wales, as 'powerful, valiant, warlike and stubborn' and in his book

Britannia, the late Professor Sheppard Frere describes them as the most successful opponents the Roman army was to encounter in these islands – holding out against the might of Rome for some twenty-five years. The Romans were also afraid of the influence of Celtic druids – spiritual and cultural leaders whose main base was in Anglesey – and, according to Welsh legend, massacred a large number of them.

Eventually, however, the Romans succeeded in establishing towns and garrisons all over the area. Their language was Latin and this was the language of government, administration, the law, construction and, later, following the adoption of Christianity as the official religion of the Roman Empire at the start of the fifth century, of religion.

Birth of the Welsh Language

Latin interacted with the native Brythonic language which morphed into Welsh around this time – in much the same way as Anglo-Saxon morphed into English under the influence of the French of the Norman conquerors some thousand years later. There are still many words of Latin origin in Welsh, especially relating to construction or the Church – such as 'pont' (bridge) or 'eglwys' (church). Interestingly, very few words of Latin origin relate to the law, indicating perhaps that native Brythonic legal systems were relatively well established before the Romans came.

Similarly, there are many words of French origin in English. Some of the most interesting show how the Norman French for many years were the master race, while the Anglo-Saxons did the menial work. For example, the Normans ate 'beef' from the French '*boeuf*', while the Anglo-Saxons tended 'cattle' (a word originating in Anglo-Saxon) in the field. Likewise they tended 'sheep' or 'pigs', while their Norman masters ate 'mutton' and 'pork' (from the French '*mouton*' and '*porc*').

It is interesting how some English people scoff at Welsh if they hear a word in a Welsh conversation which they recognise as coming from another language. They ignore – or are possibly unaware of – the fact that many English words have been borrowed from other languages too. I well remember a very superior sounding English diplomat talking on the radio about the attempts of Russian President Gorbachev to establish more friendly relations with the West towards the end of the twentieth century. The cooling of hostilities between the USSR and the West was called '*détente*' in English (a French word meaning 'easing'). The diplomat, however, warned that we should be very wary of Gorbachev's real motives. His trump card was to argue that he did not believe the Russians really believed in *détente* because they did not have a word for it in their own language!

Those dreaded mutations!

It was during the period of linguistic development as Brythonic was morphing into Welsh that 'mutations' first appeared. This is where some consonants change according to the words or sounds that precede them. This is often quoted – especially by English speakers

– as one of the supreme difficulties facing Welsh learners.

Excuse me while I have a little rant about mutations – not the Welsh ones which are fairly straightforward, but the much more complicated English ones. Perhaps you are surprised to learn that the English language contains a host of mutations too, though unlike Welsh most of the English ones come towards the end of words.

The most common is where the 't' sound becomes a 'sh' sound – for example 'create' becomes 'creation', 'donate' becomes 'donation' etc. Other examples are where the 'd' sound becomes an 's', as in 'divide' becoming 'division', and 'b' becoming 'p', as in 'prescribe' and 'prescription'.

In 'house' and 'houses' the 's' sign remains, but it is pronounced as a 'z'. 'V' can mutate into 'p', as in 'receive' and 'reception'. Interestingly, if we use the word 'receipt', the 'p' is written but not actually spoken! In a very similar word, 'deceit', the 'p' has disappeared, yet crops up again in 'deception'! The letter 'f' can become a 'v', as in 'hoof' and 'hooves'. Somewhat bizarrely it sometimes works the other way round when the 'v' sound becomes 'f' as in 'save' and 'safety'.

People also poke fun at the fact that in Welsh the letter 'f' is pronounced as the English 'v' with an 'ff' used to denote the English sound 'f'. But the 'f' is sometimes pronounced like a 'v' in English too, witness the word 'of'. If you want to say 'off' you have to use a double 'ff', as in Welsh. Sometimes 'gh' is pronounced as 'f', as in 'cough', but if you supplant the 'c' with a 'b' for 'bough', the 'gh' is pronounced like a 'w'!

Confused? I should say so. In spite of its peculiarities (and I'd hate to have to learn it from scratch!) English is a great language and can boast wonderful literature. But so can Welsh – and, at least, Welsh mutations and Welsh spellings follow clearly understandable patterns, whereas the idiosyncrasies of the English language seem to defy logic and consistency!

Anglo-Saxons

Enough of me on my hobby horse: we'd better get back to history! After the departure of the Romans in the fourth century AD, Anglo-Saxons from mainland Europe began to move into what is now England in the fifth century – originally at the invitation of the Brythonic chieftain Gwrtheyrn (Vortigern) who wanted their help in repulsing attacks from the Scots (then inhabiting present-day Ireland) and the Picts from the north. In fact, Gwrtheyrn married the daughter of the Saxon leader Hengist. It is said that to get Hengist to agree to the marriage, Gwrtheyrn had to allow the Saxons to settle in what is now the county of Kent.

According to legend, Hengist invited several hundred of Gwrtheyrn's followers to a great feast. When they were sufficiently drunk, a sign was given and the Saeson (Welsh for Saxon) drew the long knives they had hidden under their cloaks and slaughtered some three hundred Welshmen. In Welsh, this massacre is remembered as Brad y Cyllyll Hirion (the Treachery of the Long Knives). It seems we didn't learn from that experience because a Norman, William de Braose, did exactly the same thing to Welshmen living around Y

Fenni (Abergavenny) some six hundred years later as part of his campaign to cement his position as one of the most powerful Marcher Lords (Norman Lords who were a law unto themselves in the lands on the boundary between England and Wales which had been given to them by the king and over which he had little if any jurisdiction himself).

Welsh people are recognised for being very welcoming – guests are almost always offered something to drink and possibly a bite to eat. Welsh chieftains in the Middle Ages would offer visitors the best bed in the palace so that they could stay overnight and, if they visited other people, they would lay down any arms they were carrying outside as a gesture of peace and friendship. This, no doubt, is what happened at Y Fenni all those years ago and is why the Normans found it so easy to slaughter their visitors.

But, back to Gwrtheyrn in the fifth century. He is said to have retreated to the relative safety of Snowdonia where he tried to build himself a castle at a place called Dinas Emrys. But every time the castle was half-built, it would collapse. Gwrtheyrn called in a wise youth to explain this phenomenon. He is reputed to have told Gwrtheyrn that beneath the site of the castle was a vast cave where two fierce dragons, one red and one white, were continually fighting – and when they did, the earth shook and the half-built castle fell down. The youth – whose name was Myrddin, later known in English as Merlin the Magician – said the red dragon would eventually seal victory over the white one, indicating the Welsh in the end would be victorious over the Saeson – which, of course, they were in 1485. More of that later.

'King' Arthur

From the fifth century onwards, more and more Saeson began to settle in what is now called England. They were repulsed on many occasions, most notably by the legendary Arthur and his band of warriors. Very little is known for certain about Arthur but he was probably a military leader in the early sixth century incorporating both Brythonic and Roman attributes. He is credited with many victories over the Saeson, the most important of which was the battle of Mynydd Baddon in AD 516. He was eventually defeated at the battle of Camlan in 537 but nothing is known for certain about his death.

The legend grew that he was not dead, but rather

dormant, and would rise again one day when his people needed him most. The story of Arthur has been adopted by many other countries, notably England and France – where romantic notions of the Round Table and of chivalry were developed in later

King Arthur.
Picture: Margaret Jones.

years. A statue of 'King Arthur' – though there is no evidence that he ever merited that title – can be seen in the Hofkirche (Imperial Church) in Innsbruck in Austria for example. Indeed, the myth of Arthur and other Celtic legends were one of the mainsprings of medieval romantic literature across Europe.

The Saeson gradually conquered more and more of eastern Britain. There is little evidence, however, of any widespread evacuation of the area by the Brythonic people living there. Rather, they were gradually absorbed by the newcomers. Evidence of the old Brythonic language can still be found in English place names, such as Dover (dwfr = water), Avon (afon = river). They have even got more than one River Avon, which just means River River! (Permit me a little aside. One of the most amusing Anglicisations of Welsh place names is their rendering of Abermo in Meirionnydd (Meirionethshire) as Barmouth. 'Aber' means 'mouth of' and 'mo' is a contraction of the name of the river – Maw or Mawddach. Barmouth therefore means 'the mouth of the mouth', with the name of the river having been dropped entirely!)

The Anglo-Saxon settlements in England did eventually, however, drive a wedge between the unconquered Brythonic people of Wales and those in what is today south-west England and later those of northern England and southern Scotland. This marked the end of the fledgling British nation. Many people, of course, still talk as though a British nation exists today. This is nonsense. How come we play 'inter-national' matches (a contest between different nations) against each other? There is a British state, of course, comprising four nations, but the British nation died well over 1,500 years ago.

Cymry – the Welsh

The language of the unconquered Brythons of south-west England developed into Cornish and that of the Brythons of what is now Wales and north-west England and southern Scotland into Welsh. While the Anglo-Saxons called us foreigners (Welsh), we called ourselves Cymry (fellow countrymen or comrades) and our land Cymru. The Romans had made a significant impact on the country – building towns and garrisons, establishing a more ordered civic society and, of course, building new roads which all helped the Welsh tribes to gel together as Cymry. This was the beginning of a recognisable Welsh nation.

Initially the Men of the North (i.e. north-west England and southern Scotland today) were part of that nation. The name Cumbria is, of course, a variant of the name Cymru. The emerging Welsh language was spoken in those parts – indeed, there are still some remnants of the language in the way shepherds in Cumbria and parts of Northumberland and Yorkshire count their sheep today.

Patrick was a Welshman from those parts (Ystrad Clud, or what is known as Strathclyde today). He was captured and taken to Ireland as a slave. He began preaching Christianity there and was eventually made their patron saint. The first examples of Welsh-language poetry handed down to us originated in the Old North commemorating battles against the Saeson, the most notable being at Catraeth (present-day Catterick in Yorkshire).

On the western shores of Wales and the Old North, there was considerable interaction between the Welsh and the Scots who, at that time, lived in what today we call Ireland. We have already seen that Patrick went to preach Christianity in Ireland – many years before St Augustine landed in Kent to try to convert the Anglo-Saxons to the new religion. Early Welsh stories – later immortalised in written form in *Pedeir Keinc y Mabinogi* (The Tales of the Mabinogi) – include stories of inter-marriage between a Welsh princess and an Irish king and the princess's brother, Bendigeidfran, going to Ireland to bring her home because of her ill-treatment at the Irish court.

Like so many ancient tales, this in part is an attempt to explain a place name. The Irish for Dublin is Baile Átha Cliath, the Town of the Ford of Hurdles. The story says that Bendigeidfran (Blessed Brân, or Brân for short) was a giant of a man and when his army came to the River Liffey he laid across the river to enable his soldiers to cross over his body to the other side. One of the oldest of Welsh sayings is: 'A fo ben, bid bont' – 'He who would be a leader, let him be a bridge'.

Cunedda

Remnants of Irish settlements can still be seen in Sir Benfro (Pembrokeshire) and parts of Gwynedd and Cornwall. Cymry – comrades – from the Old North came down to Wales to help local princes withstand

Irish attacks and incursions. The most notable of these was Cunedda and his sons who settled here. Several members of his family – such as Meirion, Ceredig, and Edern – are remembered in the names of different areas of Wales. This left the Old North in a weakened state of defence and the Irish turned their attention more and more to present-day Scotland. Indeed, it was the Scots of Ireland who gave the country its present name, with the older inhabitants, the Picts, retreating more and more to the Highlands.

No one seems certain how Brittany became part of the Brythonic inheritance. Some Brythons may have moved across the channel to escape the marauding Irish whilst some, together with some Irish themselves, may have gone there to help convert the people to Christianity. As a result, another variant of the Brythonic language developed there which today we call Breton in English – Llydaweg in Welsh.

We have seen how the old Brythonic language had developed into three new languages – Welsh, Cornish and Breton. In a similar fashion, the other Celtic language spoken in these islands at the time of the Roman conquest – Goidelic – was developing into three new languages – Irish Gaelic, Scots Gaelic and Manx. Six new Celtic nations had emerged as a result of the collapse of the Roman Empire and the Anglo-Saxon incursions.

The Glorious 'Dark Ages'

English historians, and indeed many throughout western Europe, refer to the post-Roman period as the 'Dark Ages' largely because there is little written evidence from that time. That description, however, is certainly not true of Wales. In fact, this was a golden age for Wales, especially in terms of religion, learning, poetry and law.

Christianity

Wales was becoming a Christian country even before Constantine – a Roman general serving in Britain – declared himself Emperor of Rome at York in AD 306. He found it convenient to allow Christians to practise their faith and, by the edict of AD 313, allowed them to do so. According to some legends, the Roman road leading south from Caernarfon (the first – and only – north-south Wales highway!) is called Sarn Helen (Helen's Causeway) after Constantine's mother. It is more likely, however, that it was named after another Helen – a local girl from Gwynedd – who married Macsen Wledig, as the Emperor Magnus Maximus is known in Wales.

One of Europe's earliest colleges for training young men to go out to convert people to Christianity was established around the start of the sixth century by

St Illtud at Llanilltud Fawr in present-day Vale of Glamorgan (rather quirkily called Llantwit Major in English). This seminary taught much more than religious instruction and is regarded by some as the first embryo university in Europe.

It was from here that priests went all over Wales and to Ireland and Brittany to convert people to the new faith. They had considerable success. The groups they established in Ireland, in their turn, produced more missionaries, one of the foremost of which was Andrew who went to Scotland and later became patron saint of that country. It is interesting to note that of the four nations of the British Isles, only Wales has a patron saint (Dewi Sant or Saint David) who was a native of his country.

St George, of course, was from the Middle East and many countries, apart from England, have adopted him as their saint.

When St Augustine landed in Kent in AD 597, long after the seminary at Llanilltud Fawr was established, he tried to convert the whole of these islands to the Roman Catholic version of the Christian faith. This was resisted for a long time by

Saint David: south window of Church of Saint Padarn, Llanbadarn Fawr.

the already well-established Celtic Christian Church. It was not until the eighth century that Welsh Christians finally accepted the supremacy of the papacy in Rome.

A Thriving Literature

We have already noted the tales of the Mabinogi (popularised in the nineteenth century as the result of an English translation by Lady Charlotte Guest). These stories were very advanced for their time and, together with other Welsh tales of this time, gave rise to the myth of King Arthur and, as noted, hugely influenced the development of romantic tales across western Europe – especially in the later chivalrous guise given to them by Sieffre o Fynwy (Geoffrey of Monmouth – a Norman Welsh scholar who toured Wales recruiting volunteers for the crusades to the Holy Land in the twelfth century).

The first Welsh-language poetry we know of originates from about the sixth century (some eight hundred years before Chaucer was writing poetry in English!). Much of the poetry is comparatively easily accessible to Welsh readers today and large sections of it are extremely descriptive and moving. One set of very evocative verses which are now known as *Canu Heledd* was written down in the ninth or tenth centuries, but relates to the defeat of a prince called Cynddylan, who was Helen's brother, whose estates were destroyed by marauding Saeson in the early seventh century. Her simple description of visiting the ruins of her brother's palace is quite moving. Here are just two of the verses:

Ystafell Gynddylan, ys tywyll heno
Heb dân, heb wely:
Wylaf wers, tawaf wedy.

Ystafell Gynddylan, ys tywyll heno
Heb dân, heb gannwyll:
Namyn Duw, pwy a'm dyry pwyll?

(Cynddylan's Hall is dark tonight: no fire, no
bed. I shall weep for a while and then fall silent.
Cynddylan's Hall is dark tonight: no fire, no candle.
Who but God can keep me sane?)

Over this period, poetic forms were developed into
a system termed 'cynghanedd'.

Cynghanedd is quite unique to Wales. It can take up
to twenty-four different forms, but the basic principle is
one of strict alliteration and internal rhymes – in some
cases with consonants in the first half of a line having
to be exactly the same and come in the same sequence
and with the same stress in the second half of the line.
This calls for a very high degree of craftsmanship. It
does not always give rise to high quality poetry, but
when fused with true poetic resonance, the results can
be amazing.

'A walesi bárdok'
(Hungarian for 'The Bards of Wales')

The bards who wrote such poetry were highly respected.
In particular, they were valued by princelings and

local chiefs and were expected to compose paeans of praise to their benefactors in their courts and at their banquets. On many occasions, the bard was the only person allowed to sit in the presence of the lord. This is the origin of the custom of awarding a Bardic Chair to the winner of Eisteddfod poetry competitions – but only to those who write in the traditional twenty-four strict metres. Poets not wishing or unable to write in that form, compete instead for the Eisteddfod Crown which, to this day, has slightly less prestige attached to it.

In later years many bards began writing of more everyday occurrences that were relevant to ordinary folk in the local tavern, and they wandered from place to place across large parts of the country. The most famous of these was Dafydd ap Gwilym who wrote in the mid fourteenth century. There is no doubt that Welsh bards were pre-eminent amongst poets throughout Europe in the so-called 'Dark Ages'.

In fact, one of the most famous poems in Hungarian is 'A walesi bárdok' (The Bards of Wales). This heroic poem commemorates the occasion in the late thirteenth century when Edward I – who had waged a vicious campaign against Wales, laying waste much of the country – held a feast in Trefaldwyn (Montgomery) to which he invited a large number of Welsh bards and commanded them to sing his praises. One by one they sang of a mighty king who had laid waste to a beautiful and bountiful country which was now desolate, or a king who had entered a land of beautiful women who had been widowed, a land which had been ravaged by his troops. Each in his turn was beheaded for his affrontery. It is said that Edward became so afraid of the unrest the Welsh bards might stir up that he sent out his soldiers to kill every bard they could find. According to Welsh legend, some five hundred were slaughtered – reminiscent of the way the Romans slaughtered the Druids – because they were afraid of them!

This, therefore, was the subject matter chosen by János Arany, the most well-known Hungarian poet of the day, when the Hungarian rebellion against their Austrian masters was put down in 1848 and he was required to write a poem of praise to the Austrian Emperor – who was apparently too dim-witted to understand the irony! The Hungarians understood the significance, however, and even today every schoolchild in Hungary learns the poem by heart. Everyone I have spoken to in Hungary can recite parts of the poem. In fact, at the beginning of the twenty-first century the Hungarians invited Welsh composer Karl Jenkins to put the words to music. The striking choral work he produced was premiered in Budapest in 2011 and its second performance was given at the National Eisteddfod of Wales in Bro Morgannwg (Vale of Glamorgan) in 2012.

Amazingly, the bardic tradition lives on in Wales. Our pre-eminent festival today is not a race meeting or a football match: it is our National Eisteddfod which celebrates art and culture in all its forms. The first Eisteddfod, a gathering of poets and musicians to vie with each other for the audience's favours, was held in Aberteifi (Cardigan) in 1176. Periodic eisteddfodau followed but the festival fell into decline, especially after Wales was annexed to England in 1536. It was revived again in the early nineteenth century. It has changed significantly over the centuries, of course, and has widened its range of competitions and other events beyond all recognition. Pride of place, however, is still given to the poets and ordinary people flock to the Literary Tent to enjoy Talwrn y Beirdd – competitions for poets, many writing in the traditional cynghanedd.

Welsh Laws

Another shining example for the rest of Europe was the way in which Welsh laws were developed. Although a recognisable nation, we in Wales had not established the mechanisms of a single state. As Gwynfor Evans observed in his book *Land of my Fathers*, whereas the 'United Kingdom' nowadays is a single state comprising four distinct nations, a thousand and more years ago Wales was a single nation comprising a number of different embryonic states.

Each lord or princeling had his own court with its own support arrangements and its own laws. We have seen how the early laws adopted by Welsh chieftains were strong enough to withstand the influence of Roman law. In 909 Hywel Dda (Hywel the Good), prince of Deheubarth (comprising most of the south-western part of the country), called all the princelings and chieftains and their legal advisers together to Hendy Gwyn ar Daf (Whitland) in order to produce one set of laws for the whole country. This was done not by means of a decree from on high, but by discussion and the consent of

Part of Hywel Dda's Whitland memorial.

those participating. This was a much more important milestone in the development of democracy than the signing of Magna Carta by King John three hundred years later in 1215. That was forced on an unwilling king by the barons, and it basically looked after baronial interests rather than those of the population at large.

The laws of Hywel Dda codified in Whitland in 909 were far in advance of anything else in Europe at that time and contained many egalitarian elements. Women enjoyed a number of rights regarding personal relationships and inheritance (it took the British state over a thousand years to catch up with us on that score!). If crimes were committed, the emphasis was on restitution or compensation for the victim rather than mere retribution.

The laws were aimed at producing social harmony rather than the imposition of regal or state will. The legal historian Dafydd Jenkins describes our system as *Volksrecht* (the people's rights) as opposed to the more common *Kaiserrecht* (the king's rights).

The laws also decreed that when a person died the property and goods left behind should be divided equally amongst all the children rather than left to the first-born alone which became the English system. If a man died without heirs his property was to be distributed between the local community rather than revert to the Crown as under Norman law.

The Welsh system ensured a much more widespread distribution of property and wealth than was usual elsewhere. In one respect this can be viewed as a disadvantage in terms of the accumulation of sufficient resources to provide the engine for industrial development in later centuries. It ensured, however, that Wales developed as a much more egalitarian society than many others, a society for which questions of individual rights and social justice were very important.

Resisting the Normans

Then along came the Normans!

It is often overlooked that the Normans conquered Anglo-Saxon England very quickly, whereas it took them over two hundred years to subdue Wales! There were two main reasons for that. Firstly, the kings of Wessex had succeeded in gaining overlordship of most if not all of England. Once the Normans had killed King Harold at the Battle of Hastings in 1066, the remaining opposition was leaderless and disunited. It is, of course, something of an exaggeration – but perhaps not too much – to say that the Anglo-Saxons were beaten in a day.

Wales, however, still comprised a number of separate small kingdoms. If one of them was beaten in battle, there were plenty of others to carry on the fight. Secondly, of course, the mountainous terrain of Wales made it easier for the Welsh to resist, valley by valley, developing what we today would call the skills of guerrilla warfare.

The Princes of Gwynedd

Then along came the princes of Gwynedd! The popular view of Llywelyn the Great and his grandson Llywelyn the Last is that they were great national heroes trying to stem the tide of Normans marching on Wales. That, of course, is true and I was pleased to be able, back in 1964, to help establish what has become an annual rally at Cilmeri outside Llanfair-ym-Muallt (Builth Wells) where Llywelyn the Last was killed. It is important we remember our heroes, whatever we may think of their policies!

In my view, though I am sure this was not their intention, the princes of Gwynedd in fact did the Normans' dirty work for them. By uniting most of Wales under their banner, it meant that the Normans only had to beat them to beat the whole of Wales – and, in view of the Normans' vastly superior numerical strength, it was virtually inevitable that they would win in the end. One of the main advantages, which had sustained the struggle against the Normans for a couple of hundred years, was thrown away.

Worse than that, the princes of Gwynedd jettisoned many Welsh traditions and copied the Normans in other ways too. They tried to introduce primogeniture (i.e. the first-born inheriting everything) rather than the egalitarian Welsh system of gavelkind, by which everything was shared. They also established religious houses for those monastic orders favoured by the Normans. By and large, the Cistercian monasteries favoured the Welsh princelings against the Normans, whereas the Benedictines, brought to Wales by the Normans themselves, sided almost exclusively with the invaders. The princes of Gwynedd tried to beat the Normans by playing them at their own game. Sorry boys, it was almost bound to fail.

On the defeat of Ein Llyw Olaf (Our Last Leader,

Llywelyn's memorial at Cilmeri.

as Llywelyn the Last came to be known), Edward I of England tried diplomacy to pacify the Welsh. He promised them a prince born in Wales who could speak no English and then presented them with his own baby son, born in Caernarfon castle, who indeed fulfilled those conditions. The trick proved largely successful – and persists to this day!

Sporadic opposition did continue after the defeat of Llywelyn the Last, with uprisings such as those led by Ifor Bach on Cardiff castle and later Llywelyn Bren on Caerffili castle. The Norman attitude quickly changed from diplomacy to brutal repression. For example, as far as we are aware, Llywelyn Bren was the first man in Britain to be hung, drawn and quartered – one of the most horrendous deaths imaginable.

Owain Glyndŵr

There was little sign of a really successful opposition to the Normans, however, until Owain Glyndŵr took up the cudgels at the start of the fifteenth century. He reverted to the more traditional method of guerrilla fighting – indeed, Fidel Castro of Cuba regarded him as the first effective guerrilla leader of the last two millennia, and Castro copied many of Glyndŵr's methods in ensuring liberty for his country. Glyndŵr also favoured the traditional Welsh religious houses, while sacking many of those favoured by the Normans. For example, he spared the Greyfriars monastery in Cardiff when he sacked the settlement at the start of the fifteenth century – in part, at least, in recognition of the fact that they had given a decent burial to the remains of Llywelyn Bren's body.

Glyndŵr was also a lawyer and a statesman, making international alliances, calling an all-Wales parliament in Machynlleth in 1404, and proposing the establishment of two universities in Wales. He made alliances with disaffected English noblemen and they planned to overthrow the king and divide England and Wales between them. They marched on the king's army near Worcester but, for whatever reason, no decisive battle ensued. Owain's supply lines were weak and he withdrew his army back to Wales.

Owain freed most of Wales from the Norman yoke for a number of years but he was unable to consolidate his position and secure permanent gains. The Normans began to make inroads into the Welsh heartland and retake many of the castles Glyndŵr had captured. In the end, he disappeared and became a mystical figure – in the King Arthur mould – because no one knew what eventually happened to him. Like King Arthur, it was believed by many that he would return one day to lead his nation to victory.

Owain Glyndŵr.

In fact, he probably went to live with one of his daughters who had married into the Scudamore family of Kentchurch, just across the present Welsh border in Herefordshire, a mile or so from Grosmont in Gwent. (It is of interest to note that in that part of Herefordshire, called Archenfied in English (Ergin in Welsh), many Welsh place names persist – e.g. Bagwyll-y-Llidiart! – and Welsh was spoken so widely by many in the area that it was a condition, until the early twentieth century, that the town clerk of Hereford be a Welsh speaker.) The Scudamores were Normans who had come to Wales before the invasion of 1066 as architects and builders to erect an abbey at Abbey Dore. Remarkably, the house is still lived in by members of the same family – now a very well-known family in English sporting circles – who can point out the room in which Glyndŵr is supposed to have spent his last years.

Following the Glyndŵr uprising, Norman punishment became more collective against Welshmen as a whole, as opposed to the individual punishment meted out previously. Welshmen were not allowed to live in or even enter the Norman towns after dark; they were not allowed to carry on trade or business in the towns, or to carry arms or even to marry a Norman.

The Tudors

It is fairly common in some circles these days to denigrate the Tudors as monsters or villains – partly due to the fact that two of Henry VIII's wives were executed, and partly because some adherents of both Protestantism and Catholicism were executed under Mary and then Elizabeth for failing to renounce their faith. Such strictures, however, is to judge them by present-day standards rather than those of the age.

Whilst not exactly saints, the Tudors certainly did not indulge in many of the horrendous activities favoured by some of the Plantagenets who preceded them.

Their concern was more for the safety of the realm and (until Elizabeth, at least) the continuity of the dynasty, rather than personal possessions or aggrandisement. In fact, I would argue that the Tudors were the only effective royal dynasty England has ever had! It was they, certainly, who brought peace to England and Wales and laid the foundation of a secure, well-established state. What other royal dynasty could possibly claim to have done as much?

Henry Tudor

Back to the history! Much of the fifteenth century in England resounded to inter-family battles between the various branches of the Plantaganet dynasty crystallised around the Red Rose of Lancaster and the White Rose of York. Henry V was of the Lancastrian line and when he died his young widow married his loyal aide – a Welshman, Owen Tudor of Penmynydd, Sir Fôn (Anglesey). They supported the Lancastrians and eventually Owen Tudor's grandson, Henry, became the Lancastrian claimant to the throne of England. He met the Yorkist King Richard III at the Battle of Bosworth Field in 1485. Richard was killed and Henry picked up the crown and crowned himself as Henry VII of England. He could trace part of his ancestry back to Edward III and he later married Elizabeth of York, who was the daughter of Edward IV, to help reconcile the two warring factions. He always maintained, however, that he claimed the crown not by right of inheritance but by right of conquest – the last king of England to do so.

Initially, Henry probably considered himself more a champion of the Lancastrian cause rather than as a champion of Wales. He had been born – and spent his early years biding his time with his uncle Jasper Tudor, Earl of Pembroke – in Pembroke castle. When things became too hot for a potential Lancastrian claimant to the throne, they sought safety in Brittany. When the time was ripe, they returned to Pembroke with some French troops in support and from there they began their long march north to Aberystwyth and then east through Montgomeryshire to meet King Richard III just outside Leicester. They deliberately chose this route so as to gather as much Welsh support as possible. By the time Henry met Richard III on Bosworth Field, the bulk of his army consisted of Welshmen.

Pembroke castle.

Henry spoke Welsh and deliberately played on his Welsh heritage to rally support for his cause. Welsh poets of the time helped rouse the Welsh population, describing Henry as 'Y Mab Darogan' (the Son of Prophecy) – a reincarnation of Arthur and Owain Glyndŵr come to lead the Welsh to victory over their enemies at last. And when he was the victor at Bosworth, they thought the Normans had finally been defeated.

Defeat of the Normans

And they had been defeated, of course. Richard was the last king of French descent to wear the English crown. Indeed, ironically, the English have never had an English monarch. They had Anglo-Saxon kings before the Norman invasion, of course, but they were no more English than the Brythons were Welsh. As we have seen, Wales was created by the impact of the Romans on the native Brythons and, in the same way, England was formed by the impact of the Norman French on the native Anglo-Saxons in England. After the Norman French and the French Plantaganets on the English throne came the Welsh Tudors, the Scots Stuarts, the Dutch house of Orange, the German Hanoverians and later the German Saxe-Coburg-Gotha dynasty who decided, for diplomatic reasons, during the First World War to change their name to Windsor.

Defeating the last remnants of the Norman invasion, however, did not mean that Wales was free of domination by England. Henry did not forget his Welsh heritage. He called his eldest son Arthur after the legendary British hero; he included a Welsh dragon on the royal coat of arms; he employed a Welsh-speaking nanny for his children – as did his son Henry VIII, which is why his daughter, Elizabeth I, was able to speak some Welsh.

However, Henry's main concern was to ensure an end to civil war and, as has been noted, one of his first acts was to choose a Yorkist princess for his wife. He also incorporated both the red rose of the Lancastrians and the white rose of the Yorkists into the new Tudor rose. He found that keeping the peace between various English factions was more important to him than rewarding the Welsh for their support. Before long, the bards of Wales were mourning his new priorities:

Gwell gan Siasper a Harri

Yw gwŷr y Nord na'n gwŷr ni.

'Jasper and Henry now favour the men of the North over our men,' they wrote. To find advancement and royal favour, many ambitious Welshmen decided to seek their fortune at court in London and more and more Welshmen went to Oxford or Cambridge universities. These developments led to a greater integration between Welsh scholars and gentry and their English counterparts than had been seen previously.

Henry VIII

Henry VII's eldest son, Arthur, was married to Catherine of Aragon and was, of course, destined to succeed his father as king of England. However, he died when he was still very young and his brother, another Henry, became heir to the throne and was married to his brother's widow in order to keep relationships with Spain on an even keel. He and Catherine had a daughter – later Queen Mary – but she failed to give birth to a son which was of vital importance to Henry to ensure the future of the Tudor dynasty.

Henry VIII argued that he should never have been allowed to marry his brother's widow, and that his marriage to Catherine should therefore be annulled so that he could marry Anne Boleyn in the hope that she would give him a male heir. He petitioned the Pope but under duress from Spain the Pope refused to agree. In the end Henry unilaterally broke England's ties with

Rome and declared himself head of an independent English church.

Act of Union 1536

This gave rise to a quarrel not only with the papacy but also caused a great deal of animosity between England, Spain, France and other continental Catholic powers. Henry was therefore anxious to strengthen the security of his realm against foreign attack, mindful of the fact that his father had landed with a band of French soldiers in Pembroke to claim the English crown some forty to fifty years earlier. These were the influences which led him to introduce the Act of Union of England and Wales in 1536. This was a unilateral action on his part, without any discussion with anyone in Wales, but many Welshmen welcomed the Act as it did away with the disadvantages imposed on the Welsh following Glyndŵr's uprising and put them on an equal footing with their English counterparts in seeking positions at court and in government.

It was this Act, by the way, which created thirteen counties in Wales. They are listed in the Act and among them is Monmouthshire. No law has ever been presented, let alone passed, to change the status of Monmouthshire as one of the counties of Wales, though its boundaries have been amended from time to time. Any talk of Monmouthshire having once been part of England is pure nonsense and not based on fact. Confusion over this issue probably arose because, for administrative convenience, Monmouthshire was included in the Oxford judicial circuit. For the same reasons Chester was included in the north Wales judicial circuit, but no one to my knowledge has ever argued that Cheshire was therefore a part of Wales!

Welsh Influence at Court

Increasing Welsh influence at court and in government administration reached its peak under the reign of Elizabeth I. William Cecil (Cecil was an Anglicised version of the name of an old Welsh family called Seisyll) who never hid his pride in his Welsh ancestry, became Elizabeth's first Secretary of State and one of her most trusted advisers. He was at the heart of most of the international diplomacy in which Elizabeth found herself embroiled in her effort not to bow the knee to rival continental powers.

The quirky scientist Dr John Dee, if such a description can be applied to him, reminded Elizabeth that the Americas had supposedly been discovered by a Welsh prince, Madog, in 1170, some two hundred years before Columbus sailed west. Elizabeth needed no persuading that this gave her the right to claim sovereignty over the lands then being colonised in the new world. Indeed, it was probably Dee who coined the term 'British Empire', but he was referring to a North Atlantic Empire supposedly established by the Brythonic King Arthur, rather than the English-dominated 'British' empire of later centuries.

In spite of some of his idiosyncrasies, Dee was a learned and well-respected scholar. He was one of the first group of people to be made a Fellow of Trinity College, Cambridge, in 1546. He was invited to lecture at the universities of Paris, Reims and Oxford, and was offered a permanent professorship in both of the latter, both of which he turned down. He wrote on scientific subjects and published some of Robert Recorde's seminal works on mathematics (see later).

Another notable Welsh family – this time in early seventeenth-century London – were the Myddeltons, originally from Denbighshire. Sir Thomas Myddelton served as Lord Mayor of London and his kinsman Sir Hugh Myddelton solved the city's huge water supply problem for the burgeoning population by building a new, largely underground waterway (termed 'The New Cut') which is still carrying water to the people of London to this day.

William Morgan's Bible

Elizabeth I's most profound influence on Wales was her decree that the Bible should be translated into Welsh and made available in every church in Wales. This was probably more an attempt to bind her realm together in religious observation and allegiance rather than to support the Welsh language. William Salesbury's translation of the New Testament and the *Book of Common Prayer* were published in 1567 and a new translation of the whole Bible was published in 1588. This was by Archbishop William Morgan of Llanelwy (St Asaph). Beibl William Morgan, as it became known, appeared some seventeen years before the King James Bible became the standard English translation. William Morgan's was a masterly work. He translated parts of the Old Testament from the original Hebrew rather

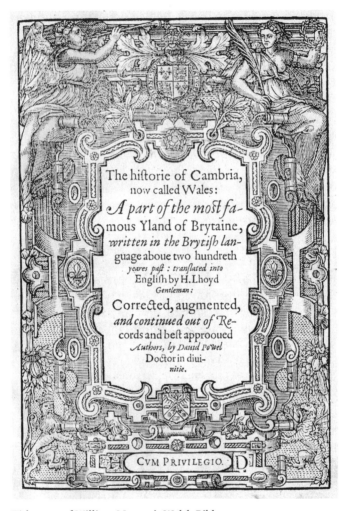

The hiſtorie of Cambria,
now called Wales:

A part of the moſt fa-
mous Yland of Brytaine,
written in the Brytiſh lan-
guage aboue two hundreth
yeares paſt : tranſlated into
Engliſh by H.Lhoyd
Gentleman :

Corrected, augmented,
and continued out of Re-
cords and beſt approoued
Authors, by Dauid Powel
Doctor in diui-
nitie.

CVM PRIVILEGIO.

Title page of William Morgan's Welsh Bible.

than the Greek or Latin versions used by many other translators. According to some accounts, he also referred to sources in Aramaic, the language spoken by Christ himself. His prose was quite exceptional. It set the standard for Welsh-language writing and ensured the survival of Welsh as a vibrant, living language.

A significant contribution was also made in this regard by Gruffydd Robert or Griffith Roberts. He was a devout Catholic who refused to acknowledge the supremacy of the Protestant religion and emigrated to Italy where he became secretary to the Bishop of Milan who was a member of the influential Borromeo family. He also found time to write the first Welsh dictionary, which was published in sections at the end of the sixteenth century. Incidentally, there is a well-known soap manufacturing company in Italy called Roberts – not a very Italian-sounding name in that form! I wonder if there is any connection?

While the future of the language had been assured for several centuries to come by these developments, Welsh national identity had been weakened by the incorporation of Wales into the English state.

It was during this period that some Welsh poets began writing in English rather than Welsh to gain a wider audience. Foremost among them were George Herbert and Henry Vaughan, both friends of the English poet John Donne. George Herbert had had a career as a scholar in Cambridge University and was appointed the university's Public Orator. He later became a Member of Parliament for a short while but then decided to give up public positions of this sort to concentrate on his religious poetry. Henry Vaughan was an influential metaphysical poet. He was less a supporter of established religion than Herbert. He related religion to nature and is regarded as one of the founding figures of Deism – that is, a belief in God as a result of rational thought rather than as an act of faith or through revelation.

Influential Welsh People

While most Welshmen of means or learning during the Tudor age sought advancement in government or in law, there were some notable exceptions. One of these was Robert Recorde of Dinbych-y-Pysgod (Tenby). He wrote the first books in English on Arithmetic, Algebra and Geometry. One significant contribution of his to the development of Mathematics might seem small to us today, but that's because we take it for granted. It was he who invented the equals sign '='. If that were to be removed mathematicians would be in real trouble. That simple invention contributed hugely to the development of the discipline.

Oliver Cromwell

With the coming of the Stuarts at the beginning of the seventeenth century and the advancement of the Scots, the dragon was removed from the royal coat of arms and Welsh people began to take more of a back seat. One of the most significant men of the period, however, was of Welsh blood – Oliver Cromwell. Through his leading role in establishing and commanding the parliamentarian New Model Army, he was instrumental in ensuring the defeat of the Royalists in the civil war of the 1640s. He was also a leading figure in the establishment of a republican government which, although it was short-lived, was instrumental in curbing the power of future British monarchs and making them, in practice, subject to the will of the people as expressed in parliament.

As his home was in East Anglia, it is often forgotten that he was in fact a member of the Williams family of Llanisien (Llanishen), then a small village a mile or two north of Cardiff, now an integral part of the city of course. His great-grandfather had changed his name to Cromwell to curry favour with his brother-in-law Thomas Cromwell, who, next to the king, was the most powerful man in England for much of Henry VIII's reign. The family retained the name Cromwell, but Oliver was well aware of his Welsh roots and in his youth even signed himself 'Oliver Cromwell alias Williams'.

As the century wore on, many Welsh people became more and more disenchanted with the somewhat haughty Anglican Church and the preponderance of Englishmen appointed to positions of influence – even in Wales itself – and responded to the appeal of Nonconformists and the Quakers. When William Penn set sail with his followers for America; he had so many Welsh people with him that he intended to call the colony he founded New Wales. This, however, was vetoed by the Stuart King Charles II and the colony became known as Pennsylvania.

The Nonconformists

The Welsh influence on America was profound in those early years. Two of the USA's most famous educational establishments, Yale University and Bryn Mawr College, have strong Welsh connections. Yale was established through the philanthropy of Welsh businessman Elihu Yale – the name probably derives from Plas-yn-Iâl, the family home in north-eastern Wales. Bryn Mawr is the name of a farm near Dolgellau where the Quakers used to meet. Many of them emigrated to America and this is where the name of Bryn Mawr College comes from.

Back in Wales, apart from the Quakers, other Nonconformist groups – like the Independents and the Baptists, and later the Methodist dissenters – gradually grew in strength. Their emphasis was more on one's personal relationship with God – on individual reading of the Bible and on prayer – rather than the ritual of the Anglican Church conducted by priests who acted as intermediaries between God and man.

This meant that congregations had to be literate and the various denominations set up Sunday schools which, apart from religious meditation and discussion, taught people to read and write – in Welsh, of course, as only a few of the gentry and a small number of scholars spoke English at that time.

A Literate Nation

However, the first to organise schools where the medium of education was Welsh was an Anglican rector, Griffith Jones of Llanddowror, Carmarthenshire. It is said he had sympathy with the Methodist movement, but was anxious not to offend some of the gentry on whom he depended for his position and some of whom helped fund his schools. In the early 1730s he began

Griffith Jones, Llanddowror.

establishing a system of 'circulating schools', primarily to teach people – adults as well as children – to read the scriptures and some of the thirty devotional books he had written himself.

Once one local group had acquired a degree of literacy, the schoolmasters would move on and establish new schools elsewhere. It is estimated that by the time of his death in 1761, about half the population of Wales had attended one of his schools, and Wales, in fact, was probably the most widely literate nation in Europe – if not the world – at the time. Catherine the Great of Russia heard about these circulating schools and commissioned a report on them so that they could be replicated in Russia. In the twentieth century, educationists faced with the daunting task of making good Fidel Castro's pledge to the United Nations to make Cuba literate within twelve months also looked to Griffith Jones's circulating schools for inspiration. They updated the system, of course, to meet their own needs in the middle of the twentieth century and in the end they produced the most widespread, successful and sustained literacy campaign the world has ever seen.

Political Thinkers

Towards the end of the eighteenth century Wales began to produce a number of influential political thinkers. The most significant, perhaps, was Richard Price who became an adviser to the British prime minister William Pitt. He was born in the Garw Valley in 1723 and became one of the leading thinkers of his age. Several of his works had a profound influence on radical thought at the end of the eighteenth century – especially, perhaps, his *Observations on the Nature of Civil Liberty* (1776) and *Observations on the Importance of the American Revolution* (1784).

He was a firm supporter of the American colonists seeking independence from England. Such was his influence that he became a friend of George Washington and he and Washington – and no one else at that time – were awarded honorary doctorates by Yale University in 1781. Price wrote extensively about the kind of government structures he thought the new United States should adopt after securing their independence in 1785. Around a third of the men who signed the American Declaration of Independence in that year, by the way, were of Welsh descent. Richard Price was also a taxation and actuarial expert (laying the actuarial basis for life insurance) and, as such, was invited by the new United States of America Congress to take charge of their Treasury – an invitation he decided to decline.

Price also welcomed the French Revolution – at least in its early days. His publication, *A Discourse on the Love of our Country* (1789), in which he enthusiastically welcomed the revolution, provoked Edmund Burke to respond with his *Reflections on the French Revolution*, a classic exposition of his Tory views. In its turn this publication triggered Tom Payne's celebrated response *The Rights of Man*. Price was held in such high regard by the French that when he died an official day of mourning was observed in Paris.

David Williams of Caerffili was another radical thinker who established a Deist chapel in London, where he abjured rules and rituals and emphasised the central importance of free thinking and of religion based on reason. Influential men such as Thomas Wedgwood, Josiah Bentley and Benjamin Franklin were regular attendees. His writings drew praise from across Europe, including from Frederick II, Voltaire and Rousseau. He elaborated his thoughts in support of American independence in *Letters on Political Liberty* (1782). This was translated into French and had a considerable impact on the thinking behind the French Revolution a few years later. Indeed, he was invited by the leaders of the revolution to help them frame a new constitution and was made an honorary citizen of France.

Gorsedd y Beirdd – The Bardic Circle

The most colourful of all the Welsh radical thinkers of the time was Edward Williams – or Iolo Morganwg to give him his bardic name – a self-taught stonemason from Llancarfan near Y Bont Faen (Cowbridge) in the Vale of Glamorgan. It is said he learned to read by watching his father carve inscriptions on gravestones! He had exceedingly wide interests, ranging from agriculture and horticulture to poetry, theology and political philosophy. He, too, was in favour of the French Revolution and hoped that something similar would take place in Wales. He is best remembered, however, for his somewhat unusual but far-reaching contribution to the cultural life of Wales.

During the eighteenth century influential Welshmen in London had gathered together to form a number of Welsh societies, the first being the Honourable Society of Cymmrodorion in 1745 (being derived from the word Cymro, meaning comrade or Welshman). Others followed, including the Gwyneddigion and

The Bardic Circle.

the Cymreigyddion. Amongst other activities they celebrated the work of Welsh poets. By the end of the eighteenth century the Gwyneddigion, hailing from northern Wales, were in the ascendancy and Iolo felt that the south was losing out. After much 'research' he 'found' a large number of manuscripts of poems by south Walians. In fact, he had written many of the poems himself and passed them off as the work of old south Wales bards. The work was of high quality and his claims were accepted at face value. Over a hundred years later scholars in the twentieth century uncovered his deception.

In tune with the age, Iolo was a romantic and he developed an interest in the old Celtic druids whom the Romans had feared so much. He re-enacted a number of druidic ceremonies (the first in 1792 on Primrose Hill in central London!). This was the origin of Gorsedd y Beirdd (the Bardic Circle) who are now a regular sight at every National Eisteddfod. As we have seen earlier, the Eisteddfod itself – which consists of competitions in a whole range of cultural activities in literature, music, performing arts, visual arts, drama etc. – had its origins in early bardic competitions where the bards competed for the honour of sitting in the Bardic Chair. As noted, the first recorded competitions of this kind go back to an Eisteddfod held in Aberteifi (Cardigan) in 1176. Local eisteddfodau were resurrected in the early nineteenth century. The Eisteddfod and Gorsedd y Beirdd were originally quite separate institutions but became fused together under Iolo Morganwg's impetus following an Eisteddfod in Caerfyrddin (Carmarthen) in 1819. The first Eisteddfod to be recognised as a 'national' festival was held in Llangollen in 1858.

The Theory of Evolution

Although Wales is often thought of as a highly religious country – especially under the influence of Nonconformity in the nineteenth century – a Welshman made a very significant contribution, indeed perhaps the vital contribution, to the development of the theory of evolution usually attributed to Charles Darwin. He was Alfred Russel Wallace, born in Brynbuga (Usk) in 1823. He developed his theory of the natural selection of species long before Darwin had published anything on the subject.

Wallace went on a specimen collecting expedition to the Amazon basin in 1848 and spent several years in Malaysia between 1854 and 1862, also collecting specimens. He corresponded with Darwin who he knew was also developing an interest in the topic. At a meeting of the Linnean Society in London in 1858, a lengthy letter from Wallace was read to those present. Its title was: 'On the Tendency of Varieties to Depart Indefinitely from the Original Type.' Darwin's friends arranged for a short summary of his views to be presented as well, fearful that the credit for the new theory would be given entirely to Wallace.

Wallace wrote many books and pamphlets, the most influential being *Contributions to the Theory of Natural Selection* published in 1870. The line demarking the boundary of flora and fauna species between Australasia and the Indonesian islands is called the 'Wallace Line' and many scientists now believe that Darwin modelled many of his ideas on those first expounded by Wallace. Darwin was more interested than Wallace in securing personal credit for the new theories and had the right social connections to ensure his success. It is somewhat ironic that the first Darwin Medal awarded by the Royal Society in 1890 was, in fact, presented to Wallace.

Development of the Nursing Profession

Another Welsh person whose contributions have been unduly overshadowed by someone else is Betsi Cadwaladr. Apart from the fact that her name is now remembered in the title of the Betsi Cadwaladr Health Board, few people know much about this pioneering nurse. Betsi was an ordinary working girl who took a job as maid to a ship's captain. She travelled all over the world and began caring for sailors who fell sick. This persuaded her to train professionally, which she did at Guy's Hospital in London. At the age of sixty-five she joined the military and was sent to Crimea, where she met Florence Nightingale. Florence was from a privileged background and the two never got on. Florence, apparently, was a stickler for rules and regulations, while Betsi got on with the job and innovated. Betsi was so frustrated with Florence's bureaucratic approach at the hospital that she left and went out to the front line to tend the wounded. In fairness, Florence later acknowledged that Betsi had been responsible for introducing many improvements to the profession.

Rather like Wallace, Betsi got on with the job – in her

case looking after the sick and wounded and developing improved nursing methods – whilst Florence Nightingale perhaps spent more time organising, publicising their work and courting publicity.

Perhaps it's not surprising that English historians tend to praise Darwin and Nightingale and forget the equally, if not more, important contributions made by the Welsh pair of Wallace and Cadwaladr.

The World's First
Industrial Nation

Whilst the Welsh people mentioned so far were very influential in their own fields, it was with the advent of the Industrial Revolution that Wales as a whole became a torchbearer on a world scale.

Man had harnessed the power of water and of fire since time immemorial, of course, to help with simple tasks such as cooking, making metal implements and weapons, and later spinning fibres and making cloth. These developments gathered pace in the seventeenth and eighteenth centuries, with larger and larger smithies and forges serving quite wide areas. The initial beneficiaries were the landowners who leased land to the entrepreneurs who invested their capital in great ironworks and in sinking coal shafts.

The Bersham ironworks in the Wrexham area were founded in 1640, but the Industrial Revolution proper sprang into life in the second half of the eighteenth century, and the greatest growth of all was located in the Heads of the Valleys of Glamorgan and Gwent, due to the plentiful local supply of iron ore, coal and limestone required for the furnaces. The Dowlais ironworks were established in 1748, followed by Hirwaun in 1757, Cyfarthfa (Merthyr Tudful) in 1765 and Blaenafon in 1788.

The French Revolution of 1789, which culminated in the execution of their king, Louis XVI, in 1793, alarmed the English government which feared revolution might spread to the British Isles. As we have noted earlier, several Welsh and English thinkers had supported its stated aims of Equality, Fraternity and Liberty. There was further and even greater cause for alarm when Napoléon (who incidentally started life as a Corsican nationalist and joined the French army in order to learn the skills with which he might fight for the island's independence!) crowned himself Emperor and began to try to spread his rule across Europe. The English took to the seas and sent armies to Spain and the Low Countries to combat his expansion.

This created a huge increase in the demand for iron for the guns, munitions and ships required to carry on the war against Napoléon. Demand for Welsh iron rocketed in the early nineteenth century. By the 1840s, the Dowlais works alone, with eighteen blast furnaces, were producing over 88,000 tons of iron a year and the total annual production in southern Wales reached 630,000 tons. Merthyr Tudful, with four of the major ironworks, soon became the largest town in Wales, and, in fact, the first large industrial town in the world.

The iron, of course, had to be exported. The River Taff was not navigable with heavy loads, so the Glamorganshire Canal was built and opened in 1794. This enabled the iron to be taken down to Cardiff for export to other countries. This was the start of the phenomenal growth of Cardiff in the nineteenth century. It soon became obvious, however, that the canals could not cope with the huge increase in trade and this was the impetus for the birth of the railways.

The Steam Train – another Welsh first

The English like to think the first train in the world pulled by a steam engine on rails was Stephenson's *Rocket* in Darlington in 1825. They somehow manage to forget that Trevithick beat him by twenty-one years and that the world's first such train – carrying both goods and passengers – ran from Penydarren in Merthyr Tudful to Abercynon in 1804. The world's first railway tunnel can still be seen just south of Merthyr town centre.

The world's first regular passenger service on rails was, in fact, the Swansea–Mumbles Tramway which opened in 1806, but the trams were initially drawn by horses rather than steam locomotives.

As the century wore on, steam powered engines pulling trains on metal railways became the main means of opening up vast areas to development in many parts of the world. This meant a further huge increase in the demand for rails from the Welsh foundries. Wherever one went in the world in the nineteenth century – from Russia to the USA – it was a fair bet that many of the railway lines came from Wales.

The Growth of the Coastal Strip

It was in Wales, too, that new and improved methods of steel production were pioneered – the Bessemer process in Dowlais in 1866 and the Siemens-Martin open-hearth process in Glandŵr, Swansea, in 1868. This meant the finished product was much more sturdy and adaptable, but it required richer ore than that available locally in southern Wales, thus requiring the import of finer quality ore from other parts of the world, notably South America, and giving a further boost to trade in the southern docks.

Eventually, of course, the owners of the steelworks realised that it made little sense to transport the ore up to the Heads of the Valleys to be turned into steel, only for the finished product to be transported back down the valleys to be exported. This led to the construction of new steelworks on the coast and was a significant element in ensuring the coastal strip of southern Wales became the main economic hub of the nation.

Newport became a very significant coal-exporting port, while in the south-west, Swansea became the world capital for copper and later nickel, and Llanelli became the world capital for tin, producing 586,000 tons a year by the 1890s. Copper had been mined in Anglesey before the Romans came but the mines had fallen into disuse. Copper, however, was now in demand again. Some say it was the copper-bottoms that began to be used for vessels of the Royal Navy in the nineteenth century which were responsible for giving Britain 'mastery of the waves' for a century or more. Anglesey copper from Mynydd Parys had a new, though comparatively brief, lease of life. Towards the end of the century Swansea was importing most of the copper it needed from Cuba and South America.

Wales also exported some of its experience and technical skill to other countries. Welsh steel workers were in great demand in the new steel industry in America, for example. Most went to the industrial parts of northern USA, and substantial remains of the plant which supplied most of the cannons and munitions for the Confederate Army in the American Civil War can still be seen in Richmond, Virginia. The plant is named after the Welsh town of Tredegar.

Russia was interested in tapping into Welsh expertise too, and John Hughes of Merthyr Tudful was given a contract by the Tsar to establish the steel industry in what is now Ukraine. He took a considerable number of Welsh workers with him to the town which was named Hughesovka in his honour. Hughes also opened a number of coal mines to provide the energy for his new steelworks. Some descendants of the Welsh workers can still be found in the city – now the largest in the industrial part of Ukraine known as the Donbas (the basin of the River Don). Today, the city is called Donetsk but it still commemorates its founder, John Hughes.

Coal

The worldwide market for iron and steel and the development of railways and later of ships powered by coal created a huge demand for Welsh coal and it began to be mined directly for export rather than to power local industries alone. Coal in the Rhondda valleys was mined mainly for this purpose.

It also gave rise to the growth of Barry as a port. One of the foremost coal barons was David Davies – who hailed from the village of Llandinam in Powys.

He objected to paying fees to the Bute family for the use of the docks they had built in Cardiff. The Butes had grown to be one of the richest families in the world by marrying into the Welsh land-owning family, the Windsors – long before the English royal family adopted the name! To get around their stranglehold on the docks in Cardiff, David Davies built his own port in Barry and, by the peak exporting year of 1913, it was exporting more coal than its bigger rivals.

Northern Wales

The industrial area of north-eastern Wales also prospered. It could never rival the burgeoning industries of southern Wales but it was more fortunate in some respects. The industrial scene there was more diversified and could therefore weather future downturns in economic activity more successfully than was possible in the valleys of southern Wales.

North-west Wales became the foremost slate producing area of Europe and many of Europe's finest buildings of the nineteenth century were roofed with slates from Blaenau Ffestiniog, Llanberis or Bethesda. The industry was dealt a blow from which it never recovered by the refusal of the quarry-owner Lord Penrhyn – who had built himself a fabulously expensive castle near Bangor on the back of their labours – to negotiate with the workers on pay and conditions. Instead, he implemented a lockout which lasted from 1900 to 1903. This is still remembered in the area and locals can still point out where the scabs and their families lived. Attempts, of course, were made to

Penrhyn slate quarry.

revive the industry after the lockout ended, but by then slate had to compete as a roofing material with less expensive tiles and the slate industry never recovered its pre-eminent position.

The Struggle
to Improve Conditions

The new industrial age, of course, brought huge social problems. A few – the landowners, the investors, the engineers – made considerable fortunes, but life was hard for those who had to do most of the work. Men, women and children spent long hours in terrible and unhealthy conditions. One little girl of five years of age worked in a pit in Merthyr for twelve hours a day. Her job was to open and shut the doors underground to let the laden wagons pass. She had a candle and a little bag of food to keep her company, but the air rushing through as the door opened blew her candle out. She spent most of her time in complete darkness and the rats ate her food. Later, the Factory Acts banned the employment of women and children underground – but the practice often persisted long afterwards when the mine inspectors were not around.

There was little concern for the safety of the workers – if any were injured or killed, there were plenty more to take their place. It was said the coal-owners took greater care of the horses which were used for dragging wagons underground than they did of their workers – for the simple reason that horses were more costly to replace! The situation in the ironworks was little better with hard manual labour, often in sweleringly hot conditions, and scant regard for human safety when handling red-hot molten metal. Workers and their families were crammed into unsanitary, overcrowded buildings and were often paid in tokens which had to be used in shops and pubs run by the works or mine-owners themselves where the price of everything was marked up to make even more profit for the bosses.

The 'Red Flag' is born

Conditions like these caused tremendous personal hardship for almost every working family and eventually led to murmurings of unrest. Things boiled over in the 1820s with the advent of groups of men roaming the industrialised areas attacking the property of steel-barons and coal-owners. They became known as 'Scotch Cattle' – no one seems to know quite how or where the name originated. Their activities were somewhat sporadic but in 1831 the workers in Merthyr Tudful took more organised action. They downed tools and demonstrated in a demand for better working wages and improved working conditions. The military were sent in to teach the demonstrators a lesson. But they were not to be cowed. They adopted the slogan 'Bread or Blood', dipped a rag in sheep's blood and waved it as a banner to rally around – and so the Red Flag was born and is now used all over the world as a symbol of the workers' fight for better conditions.

The Merthyr uprising also gave Wales its first working-class martyr – Richard Lewis, or Dic Penderyn as he was known. He was charged with wounding one of

Dic Penderyn's grave.

the soldiers brought in to quell the riots. In fact, Dic was quite innocent of the charge. The mentality that 'anyone will do' as a scapegoat, as an example to cow others or to improve police detection rates has, of course, lived on – witness the many false convictions for murder that have taken place in Wales, let alone the rest of Britain, in the twentieth century. In spite of huge protests, Dic was hanged for murder. His dying words were: 'O Arglwydd, dyma gamwedd' (O Lord, what an injustice). Thousands of people accompanied his body from Cardiff, where he had been hanged, to the burial in his home town of Aberafan. Years later, one of the rioters who had escaped to America confessed that he was the one who had caused the soldier's injury.

The Chartists

The suppression of the Merthyr uprising gave the mine-owners and ironworks-owners a little respite. But not for long. Groups of men began to organise once more and to liaise with workers in parts of England. Great hopes were pinned on the 1832 Reform Act, but when passed it extended voting rights only to adult males with substantial property assets. The workers began to develop a six-point Charter which demanded: universal male suffrage, a secret ballot, electoral constituencies of comparable populations, annual parliamentary elections, payments for MPs, and abolishing the property qualification for candidates – the latter two, of course, to enable ordinary working folk to stand for election.

All demands except annual parliamentary elections were eventually conceded, but they were regarded as far too revolutionary at the time. The Charter was presented to parliament by way of a petition in 1839, and again in 1842 and 1848, but was overwhelmingly rejected every time. The Chartists in Wales – particularly around Carmarthen, the Severn Valley around Llanidloes (centre of the wool industry – incidentally it was in Newtown in the Severn Valley some years later that the world's first mail order catalogue was produced – signs of things to come!) and the industrial valleys and towns in south-eastern Wales – felt that a tougher campaign was needed.

They organised a huge march on Newport in 1839. Some five thousand took part. Some say the intention was to stop the scheduled train to Birmingham as a signal for Chartists in the English Midlands to join the uprising. Other local leaders of the movement dreamed of creating a democratic enclave in the area. However, the authorities got wind of the planned march and armed soldiers were stationed inside the Westgate Hotel in the middle of Newport. When the marchers arrived, the soldiers opened fire, killing some twenty of them.

The leaders were arrested and sentenced to death. To try to prevent further trouble, the death sentences were commuted to transportation. One of the leaders was John Frost, who had been a Justice of the Peace and Mayor of the town. His name lives on in John Frost Square, but in an outrageous piece of vandalism the City Council sanctioned the destruction of a huge evocative mosaic mural at the entrance to the square which depicted the scene outside the Westgate Hotel when the soldiers fired on the marchers – another sad example of our lack of respect for our history.

Following the Newport massacre, the Chartists in Wales, like their counterparts elsewhere, concentrated more on political activity – organising meetings, writing pamphlets etc. – in a campaign to get the Charter officially accepted. This was the first attempt to establish a political group specifically to represent the working class. This led at the end of the century to the formation of the Independent Labour Party – whose first MP, Keir Hardie, represented Merthyr Tudful and Aberdâr (then one constituency) in Westminster.

The Daughters of Rebecca

Unrest was not confined to the industrial areas of Wales. Conditions were becoming increasingly hard in the countryside in the aftermath of the Napoleonic Wars – especially as it became more and more necessary to drive livestock miles across country to market, and to bring in supplies not available locally – e.g. limestone to improve the fertility of the soil. The roads needed improving – and many landowners began to make the roads a bit better. But, of course, there was a price to pay. The landlords put up gates to block the passage of goods and animals and demanded payment every time the gates were opened.

This proved too much for the farmers of west Wales and they began to burn and destroy the gates in protest. They took a verse from the Bible, saying that the daughters of Rebecca would seize the gates of their opponents and the men dressed up as women to avoid recognition. The protests began in Efail-wen near St Clears in Carmarthenshire in 1839 and continued for some ten years, spreading to other parts of mid Wales. The disturbances became known as the Rebecca Riots and nearly two thousand troops were sent in to suppress them.

The 'Tithe Wars'

Tenant farmers also objected to the ten per cent tithe they were expected to pay to the Church of England – especially as the vast majority of them were Nonconformists. For centuries the tithes were usually paid in kind – hence the number of tithe barns where the farmers were required to deposit a tenth of their produce for the use of the Church. In 1836, however, it was decreed that from thenceforth tithes had to be paid in cash and this put a heavy additional burden on the farmers.

In the latter part of the nineteenth century farmers in Denbighshire began to refuse to pay this levy. Bailiffs were sent in to sequester their goods which were then put up for sale at local auctions. Potential purchasers – some willingly, others no doubt fearful of retribution if they tried to buy the sequestered goods – refused to bid. The stand-off became known as the Tithe Wars and spread to other parts of northern and mid Wales.

In 1891 it seemed that a great victory had been won when the government decreed that in future the tithes should be paid by the landlords rather than the tenant farmers. The latter's joy was short-lived, however, as the landlords realised they could recoup the money they lost simply by increasing rents. Unrest continued and became much more political in nature. It was one of the issues championed by the Liberal Party in Wales – including the rising political figure of David Lloyd George – resulting ultimately in 1914 in the Disestablishment of the Church of England in Wales – although the actual constitution for the Church in Wales was not finalised until 1920. This meant that no further tithe levies were imposed on Welsh landowners.

The pattern had been set, therefore, in both the industrial and the rural parts of Wales for grievances to be pursued initially by means of direct action to be followed later by more concerted political action to remove the causes of those grievances.

Social Repercussions

Immigration and Emigration

The problems encountered in the rural areas in the nineteenth century and the huge expansion of heavy industry in southern and north-eastern Wales had a profound effect on Welsh society and on the Welsh language.

Since the mid seventeenth century considerable numbers of Welsh people had been emigrating in search of a better life. In the early years this was motivated, to a considerable extent, by the desire not to have to conform to a religion approved by the state – hence the large number of Quakers who emigrated to America. As we have seen, so many Welsh people went there under William Penn's leadership that Penn wished to call the territory where they settled 'New Wales'. The king, Charles II, intervened however, and vetoed this proposal. Instead the territory was named after Penn himself as Pennsylvania. In the eighteenth century, and even more so in the nineteenth century, the prime motivation was to escape the economic hardships in Wales and to build a new life elsewhere.

The Welsh immigrants in America wished to retain their own language and traditions – building their own chapels where the language of the services was Welsh, holding eisteddfodau and cymanfaoedd canu (hymn-singing festivals) – some of which still exist today – and producing a number of Welsh-language periodicals. The original constitution of the state of Wisconsin was written in Welsh. Yet the Welsh were also ready to immerse themselves in the social lifestyle of their new country.

As we have seen, some third of the signatories of the American Declaration of Independence were of Welsh descent. In more recent times prominent figures of Welsh descent include John L. Lewis, leader of the American mineworkers' union and one of the most powerful trade union leaders the country has ever seen.

Another prominent Welshman, whose family were Welsh speakers from Carno in Montgomeryshire, was the gangster Llewelyn Morris Humphreys, who became Al Capone's right-hand man and was known as 'Murray the Hump'. Unlike his more illustrious boss, he was never brought to trial. He was a consummate wheeler-dealer and is credited with ensuring that American trades unionists backed J.F. Kennedy to secure the presidency of the USA. Quite an influential guy!

Y Wladfa

By the middle of the nineteenth century there was a growing feeling that a permanent, new and specifically Welsh home should be found for those wishing to leave the old country to seek a better way of life. Various locations were considered – including Palestine, as many of the place names of that area were familiar to Welsh chapel-goers from their Bible readings (thank goodness that idea never came to fruition!). Eventually, they decided on Patagonia, in the southernmost part of Argentina – partly because the indigenous population was very small and the Argentinian government, which was anxious to settle the area, offered them a number of economic inducements.

A ship called the *Mimosa* with around one hundred and sixty Welsh emigrants on board sailed from Liverpool and landed in Patagonia in 1865. A small colony (Y Wladfa in Welsh) was established near the Atlantic coast. The terrain was arid and extremely difficult to farm. The settlers built a vast system of irrigation canals on which the area still depends today. Some years later an offshoot settlement was established in the foothills of the Andes, hundreds of miles to the west. It is interesting to note that in the Welsh communities of Y Wladfa, for the first time

The *Mimosa*.

in the world, women had the right to vote as well as men. Although large numbers of other migrants later settled in these areas, many people retained the Welsh language and customs. Eventually, they all had to learn Spanish – the official language of Argentina – but to this day a sizeable number still speak Welsh as well, and the teaching of Welsh in the schools of Y Wladfa is supported by the Welsh government. In addition, Welsh eisteddfodau are still common in Y Wladfa – as they are, of course, amongst people of Welsh descent in the USA. The Eisteddfod – as a concept, though not in language – is also so common in parts of Australia that it is no longer considered to be a particularly Welsh phenomenon there!

At the start of the twentieth century there was a move to transfer the Andes area of western Patagonia from Argentina to Chile. This would have meant that the two Welsh settlements – the one near the coast and the other in the foothills of the Andes – would find themselves in two separate countries. A referendum was held in the area and the Welsh campaigned to keep the whole of Patagonia in Argentina. It was successful and the president of Argentina visited Y Wladfa to thank the Welsh for their support; he addressed a meeting in the town of Gaiman – in a hotel (built by my great-grandfather!) which is now a college of music.

Internal Migration

Emigration from Wales, however, was on nothing like the scale experienced by Ireland. Migration was possibly just as big a phenomenon here as in Ireland but, whereas the absence of heavy industry in Ireland meant that those leaving home to seek a better life had little option but to emigrate overseas, the mushrooming industries of southern and north-eastern Wales meant that countryside dwellers in other parts of Wales only had to move a few score miles or so eastward to find work.

This meant that even up to the end of the nineteenth century the Welsh language remained the predominant language in all parts of the country – apart from southern Pembrokeshire, where groups from continental Europe had settled centuries before and had never learned the language. Elsewhere, Welsh-language chapels and periodicals proliferated. One of the finest Welsh-language poets of the nineteenth century, whose epic poetry has been compared to that of Milton, was a certain William Thomas from the lower Sirhowy Valley in Gwent. His attachment to his local area was emphasised by his choice of bardic name – Islwyn.

Apart from people moving into the industrialised areas from rural Wales, there were also increasing numbers of immigrants from the English West Country coming to work in the steelworks and coal mines. In general, they were absorbed into the local community and soon learned to speak Welsh themselves. The Industrial Revolution initially saved the Welsh language by ensuring that the bulk of Welsh speakers could stay in Wales rather than emigrate overseas like the Irish, who virtually lost their language.

Anglicisation

Things, however, became very different towards the end of the nineteenth century. The demand for labour in the heavy industries in southern Wales could no longer be met by inward migration from the rural parts of the country, and more and more people flooded in from England. Cardiff became the largest coal-exporting port in the world and it was in the city's Coal Exchange that the world's first million-pound cheque was written – on behalf of the US Navy for supplies of Welsh coal, then recognised as the best in the world. Ships sailed from the ports of southern Wales to all parts of the world. They were manned by seamen from a wide variety of different countries and Tiger Bay in Cardiff housed the most cosmopolitan population in Britain. It was here the first mosque was built in Britain, and Cardiff is still home to the only purpose-built Greek Orthodox church in these islands.

Substantial numbers of new immigrants married into Welsh families and learned to speak Welsh. Within living memory a gentleman whose first language was Italian learned to speak first Welsh and then English in Merthyr Tudful. As he grew older and his memory began to fail, he lost his use of English but could still understand both Italian and Welsh.

The ability of the local community to absorb immigrants, however, began to weaken and the newcomers themselves found they could get by well enough without learning the Welsh language. From the beginning of the twentieth century onwards, the proportion of the population who could speak Welsh began to decrease at an ever-accelerating pace, especially in the industrialised areas.

The second half of the twentieth century brought, at first, a trickle but later quite a considerable stream of English people moving to Wales to retire or to seek a better way of life than that offered by urban conurbations. Whilst there were honourable exceptions, of course, the bulk of these newcomers saw no need to become assimilated into the local community – indeed many seemed to think that the local Welsh community should change its ways and its language just to make life simpler for them!

Our experience in Wales has, perhaps, given us an understanding of the problems associated with immigration that people in England are only recently trying to come to terms with. We have never opposed immigrants per se. If they want to become part of our community and respect our society and language, few Welsh people have a problem with that. When immigrants do not want to assimilate with the local community, do not respect its social values, its religion and its language and want the local community to conform to the incomers' language and traditions instead that is when problems arise. We have been grappling with such problems for over a hundred years in Wales, while many English communities are only just beginning to realise what it can be like to be made to feel a foreigner in your own country.

The New Social Contract

From the middle of the nineteenth century onwards there has been a growing consensus in western society – apart, that is, from the USA – that the role of government is not merely to look after state security and to fight crime, but also to play a role in ensuring a more healthy, just and equitable society. Welshmen have been at the forefront of many of these initiatives.

We have noted how Welshmen such as Richard Price and David Williams influenced progressive thought not only in Britain but also in America and France. Someone of a more practical bent was Robert Owen of Newtown in Montgomeryshire who pioneered the concept of enterprises run co-operatively by their workers. He established factories based on these principles, first in Scotland and subsequently in the USA. He was, in fact, the father of the international co-operative movement which many people today see as the answer to the excesses of exploitative capitalism.

Education

Throughout the nineteenth century unrest amongst both the industrial and the agricultural workers of Wales helped provide the impetus for constitutional reform. It also led indirectly to the establishment of higher education in Wales before such developments took place in England. This came about because the government of the day decided that discontent could be countered better by education than by penal repression – 'Send in the schoolmaster rather than the troops' was the cry. One inquiry resulted in a report which is known in Welsh as 'Brad y Llyfrau Gleision' (The Treachery of the Blue Books) – an echo perhaps of Brad y Cyllyll Hirion 1,400 years earlier!

The report placed most of the blame for discontent in Wales not on the appalling social and economic conditions the bulk of the population suffered, but on the fact that the people spoke Welsh rather than English (the English have always found it difficult to understand that not everyone wants to be an Englishman)! The schools subsequently established under a series of Education Acts from 1870 on were a powerful Anglicising influence. Monoglot Welsh-speaking children caught speaking their own language were caned at the end of the school day and children were encouraged to avoid this punishment by incriminating others instead. I know, because this happened to my own father in Blaenau Ffestiniog in Meirionnydd (Meirionethshire).

In fact, the percentage of people who could read and write from the eighteenth century onwards was higher in Wales than in England. As we have seen, this was partly due to the circulating schools of Griffith Jones in the eighteenth century, work which was carried on by Nonconformist Sunday schools in the nineteenth century. In England, these schools acted mainly as a sort of crèche, keeping children occupied on a Sunday afternoon. In Wales, however, people of all ages attended Sunday school and one of their main functions was to make people literate so that they could read the Bible and think for themselves rather than rely passively on religious ceremonials and the teachings of the clergy. The Anglican Church opened St David's College, Llanbedr Pont Steffan (Lampeter), in 1827 to train young men for the priesthood. They also opened Trinity College, Caerfyrddin (Carmarthen), in 1848 to train teachers.

Establishing our University

Quite apart from what some regard as Europe's first embryonic 'university' in Llanilltud Fawr around the early part of the sixth century, left to our own devices we would certainly have had one, if not two, universities at the start of the fifteenth century under Owain Glyndŵr's proposals. We had to wait, however, until the second half of the nineteenth century for our first modern university to be established. And it was a very special university – not founded like most others in the world by a monarch or a government or a wealthy benefactor. It was established with the 'pennies of the miners, steelworkers, quarrymen and farmers' who clubbed together in an amazing co-operative effort to raise enough funds to establish the first college of the university in Aberystwyth in 1872.

It later developed as a federal university with colleges in Cardiff, Bangor and Swansea, together with the Medical School in Cardiff. Its main remit was to educate the youth of Wales and enable them to contribute to the development of our national life. All of the original constituent colleges have now become independent universities. It is so sad to see that few of the university establishments now scattered throughout Wales seem to share the original aims of our national university. Colleges seem to be run mainly as businesses, with the accent on attracting more foreign students rather than providing a service to the people of Wales. Increasing numbers like this boosts the ego of many a university bigwig – and probably does no harm to the size of their salaries – but it is not always clear how Wales itself benefits from such expansion. St David's College became part of the University of Wales in 1971 and Trinity College followed in 2004. The two colleges later merged and are now the nucleus of what remains of the University of Wales.

International Involvement

The interest in international affairs demonstrated by Richard Price and David Williams continued throughout the century and it was a Welshman, Henry Richard from Tregaron in Cardiganshire, who was one of the first pioneers of the concept of international mediation and co-operation replacing war as a means of settling international disputes. He persuaded a conference at the end of the Crimean War to declare that when international disputes arose, attempts should be made to resolve them by arbitration rather than resorting to war – the first such international declaration. He was elected Liberal MP for Merthyr

Tudful and Aberdâr in 1868 and – against opposition from Prime Minister Gladstone – he persuaded the Commons to endorse this policy and he argued persistently for some form of international League of Nations to tackle such issues.

He became known as 'The Apostle for Peace'. I am sure he would not be satisfied with the rather toothless United Nations organisation we have today whose decisions are continually ignored by states such as the USA and Israel. Of course, it is not really an organisation of nations at all, but rather one of state governments often representing several different nationalities. Perhaps that is its major weakness.

The introduction of universal male suffrage and secret voting in the latter part of the nineteenth century broke the monopoly of the landowners on political power. This enabled the Welsh – Welsh men, at least (women had to wait until after the First World War to secure the right to vote) – to express their preference in the ballot box. That preference in Wales has always been for what were perceived to be radical or progressive parties, with the Tories never winning a majority of parliamentary seats in our country. And of course it was a Welsh constituency (Merthyr Tudful and Aberdâr) that elected Keir Hardie in 1900 as the first MP specifically representing the working classes – he was also a strong supporter of self-government for Wales, by the way.

There were a number of prominent Welsh radical leaders, among them William Abraham, or Mabon as he was known, who was an influential figure amongst coal miners and one of our first prominent trades union leaders. He became the first president of the South Wales Miners' Federation and helped to write *The Miners' Next Step*, which advocated public ownership of the mines on a decentralised, 'syndicalist' basis. He was later elected as an MP – initially as a Lib-Lab representative, but later for Labour when it became a stand-alone political party.

Trades Unions and the Labour Party

Wales, in fact, played a crucial role in the development of effective trades unions and the establishment of the Labour Party to represent their interests. The turning point was when workers on the Taff Vale Railway went on strike in 1900 for improved wages. The owners brought in blackleg workers and took the men's union to court for loss of profits. The coal-owners won the case and the union had to pay compensation of £23,000 and costs of £25,000 – huge sums in those days. This helped persuade the unions that they needed stronger representation in parliament than was provided by labour sympathisers within the Liberal Party.

The Labour Party was formed and by 1906 it had twenty-nine MPs who managed to force through the Trade Disputes Act that year. This overturned the previous decision that owners could sue workers for going on strike and also legalised peaceful picketing.

David Lloyd George

The most prominent Welshman of all, of course, at the turn of the nineteenth / twentieth centuries was David

Lloyd George who became arguably the most effective British prime minister of all time. He made his name arguing against the levy of tithes by the Church of England and was elected Liberal MP for Caernarfon Boroughs in 1890 – a seat he retained until 1945. He campaigned for the disestablishment of the Church of England in Wales, which was eventually achieved in 1914 as a result of the Welsh Church Act. In the tradition of Henry Richard, he argued against British participation in the Boer War – a very unpopular stance to take amidst the imperialistic jingoism of the time and, in one instance, he had to leave a packed public meeting in Birmingham in disguise to avoid causing a riot.

He was a man of such charisma and with such great powers of oratory however that he could not be ignored and was promoted to a cabinet post as President of the Board of Trade in the Liberal government of 1905. He was appointed Chancellor of the Exchequer in 1908. His so-called 'People's Budget' of 1909 provoked huge opposition from the Tories in Parliament and was vetoed twice by the House of Lords. This led to the weakening of the powers of the Lords and the assertion of the supremacy of the House of Commons.

As Chancellor, Lloyd George had introduced the Old Age Pensions Act in 1908 – initially only five shillings a week, but still enough to keep the wolf from the door in those days. Following the weakening of the powers of the Lords, he was able to establish for the first time a system of unemployment benefits for those out of work. These measures were the beginning of the drive to establish a responsible welfare system for those not able to work and provided the background against which Beveridge would later produce the proposals which led to the welfare reforms instituted by the Labour government after the end of the Second World War.

Lloyd George initially opposed British participation in the First World War – again a very unpopular stance – recognising that it was a squabble between imperialistic powers with no great principles at stake for ordinary people. Once Britain was at war, however, he felt that it should be prosecuted as effectively as possible. He was appointed Minister for Munitions in 1915 – a really hot potato at that time as the British forces could not match those of Germany in terms of the weapons and munitions available to them.

He had such an impact that he was made Secretary of State for War in July 1915 and in 1916 succeeded Lord Asquith as prime minister. He provided the kind of inspirational leadership which Winston Churchill was to display in the Second Word War, and it is probably for this that he is best remembered. Unlike Churchill, who failed to retain the premiership after the Second World War, Lloyd George remained prime minister after the First World War ended – but as head of a coalition in which the Tories had a majority. He failed to achieve a great deal during this period and the Liberal Party rapidly began to decline as a political force.

Like Churchill, Lloyd George made some decisions which, in hindsight at least, had the most unfortunate consequences. There were three significant errors of judgement which have had very serious repercussions.

The first was his agreement in 1916 to the publication of the Balfour Declaration, which promised a homeland to the Jews in Palestine without any consultation with the people of Palestine themselves which has, of course, led to one of the most intractable problems of modern times in the Middle East.

Secondly, he was a party to the Treaty of Versailles at the end of the First World War which imposed very tough conditions on Germany. Some say he coined the phrase 'We must squeeze the Germans till the pips come out', though others credit the saying to Churchill. In fairness to Lloyd George, some historians have argued that, but for his input, the conditions might have been harsher still. It is now generally recognised that the conditions finally imposed on Germany were in large part responsible for the economic chaos the country suffered in the 1920s and 1930s which in turn helped create a ripe breeding ground for the extremist views and policies of the Nazis.

Lloyd George had been a supporter of 'Home Rule All Round' for the nations of Britain. Gladstone had tried more than once to secure Home Rule for Ireland, partly to satisfy Irish demands and partly to maintain the support of Irish MPs in Westminster. On each occasion he had failed. Lloyd George successfully steered through parliament the Bill creating the Irish Free State after the war. This did not satisfy all strands of Irish opinion, however, and civil war ensued in Ireland. To try to quell the dissent, Lloyd George sanctioned the use of the 'Black and Tans' – a force containing prison inmates released for that purpose. Many instances of brutality were reported wherever they went and Lloyd George's name was severely blackened in Ireland as a result.

These examples show us the danger when trying to resolve intractable problems of creating new problems to take their place. However, looking at the wider picture of what he did achieve as well as what he tried to achieve, both at home and in international affairs, few if any other British prime minister can be said to have achieved as much as Lloyd George.

Post First World War

After the First World War it was not long before the Labour Party achieved a dominant position in Welsh politics – a position it has maintained, with various degrees of supremacy, ever since. It was not long after the war, however, that a new political party emerged on the scene: Plaid Genedlaethol Cymru (the National Party of Wales), later to become known simply as Plaid Cymru. It was established at the National Eisteddfod in Pwllheli in 1925 when a small group of people from Penarth in south Wales joined forces with an equally small group based in the slate quarrying areas of north Wales.

This was a fusion of cultural nationalists, concerned

at the decline in the percentage of Welsh speakers and for the continuation of a distinctively Welsh community, with a group more attuned to the needs of the poorer working classes. As a result, Plaid Cymru developed – unlike many nationalist parties elsewhere in the world which often seem to have been royalist and right wing – a belief in equality, both within and between communities. They defined the nation as a community of communities and argued that the international order should be a community of nations prepared to co-operate together and resolve any disputes peacefully via a true inter-national organisation that would not be bullied by the big powers.

These ideas are completely in line with the principles preached – and where possible practised – by the bulk of influential Welsh thinkers throughout our history. In terms of rhetoric, there have been wide differences between the Labour Party and Plaid Cymru down the years – the former based on philosophic and economic concepts, while the latter is based more on traditional Welsh values. In practice, however, their basic principles are much more closely aligned. Both are 'internationalist', with Labour supporters sometimes seeming to believe that this supplants what they would regard as narrow nationalism. Plaid Cymru, on the other hand, believes that true internationalism, by its very name, is something which must be based on nations free to run their own national life as they see fit, but co-operating together with other nations for the common good.

If one recognises that the basis of capitalism is a system where money is king – where money, in fact, controls people – whilst socialism is a system where people control money and places the common good above individual profit and exploitation, there is no doubt (well, at least there was no real doubt until Tony Blair came along) that both Labour and Plaid came down on the same side of the fence.

Post Second World War

Great strides were made by the Labour government after the Second World War to build on the socially inclusive policies brought in by Lloyd George in the days before the First World War. It is interesting to note the role of Welshmen in this enterprise: most notable of all, of course, was Nye Bevan who founded the National Health Service – based at least in part on his experience of community health service provision organised and funded by the workers in his home town of Tredegar. In many ways, this was a local co-operative venture which Bevan turned into a national institution which is still today, in spite of all its difficulties and attempts by politicians to privatise large chunks of it, the most comprehensive and cost effective health system in the world. The other great innovation was that of a comprehensive National Insurance scheme – again, with another Welshman at the helm, this time Jim Griffiths, MP for Llanelli.

To my mind, the involvement of Welshmen in these developments is no fluke or coincidence: their attitudes and policies are rooted in our history. All our major thinkers have been radicals, our people have always voted predominantly for what we perceive to be radical parties. When we have had the opportunity to make laws or take decisions in social matters, we have almost always favoured equality and social justice over other considerations. It is also worthy of note that when a Welsh National Assembly was eventually established as a result of the 1997 referendum, it scored a world first even before its first meeting – it was the first such body in the world where there were as many women as men and, within a couple of years, women were in the majority in the Cabinet – another world first!

Leisure, the Arts and Sciences

Wales's contribution, of course, has not been limited to promoting social equality and a just society. Welsh men and women have been prominent too in sports, entertainment and the arts and sciences. It is scarcely necessary to mention the game which has come to be identified with Wales – rugby. Barry John was universally recognised as the 'King'. His half-back partner Gareth Edwards has been voted the best rugby player ever, while players like Bleddyn Williams, J.P.R. Williams, Gerald Davies and Shane Williams are among the world's greatest players. Our national rugby stadium, of course, is the best in the world. Not to be outdone, football has given us internationally recognised 'greats' like John Charles, Ian Rush, Ryan Giggs and Gareth Bale.

In music, Tom Jones, Shirley Bassey, the Manic Street Preachers, the Stereophonics and the Super Furry Animals are international stars. In the classical field our international opera stars have included

Geraint Evans, Gwyneth Jones, Stuart Burrows, Margaret Price, Dennis O'Neill and Bryn Terfel – all of whom have starred in opera houses throughout the world. Our famous actors include Richard Burton, Siân Phillips, Anthony Hopkins, Ioan Gruffudd, Rhys Ifans, Michael Sheen, Matthew Rhys and the actor/ playwright Emlyn Williams.

Our poets – apart from the large number writing in Welsh – include some of the best poets writing in English, such as Dylan Thomas, Vernon Watkins, R.S. Thomas and Dannie Abse. We have produced internationally renowned composers like Grace Williams, Ivor Novello, Daniel Jones, William Mathias and Alun Hoddinott. Our painters have included Richard Wilson, Thomas Jones (Pencerrig), Augustus and Gwen John and Kyffin Williams and due to the generosity of the Davies sisters (granddaughters of the David Davies who established the docks in Barry) our National Museum and Art Gallery houses the finest collection of Impressionist paintings outside Paris.

Our, at first, amateur national opera company was established in 1946. It carved an international reputation for itself and later became fully professional. We established the world's

Bryn Terfel.

first National Youth Orchestra in 1948. We also established the world's first Children's Commissioner, followed shortly afterwards by the first Older People's Commissioner – trying to protect the rights of some of the most vulnerable in our society in this increasingly complex age.

We have also produced four Nobel Prize winners: Clive Granger of Swansea for Economics, Brian Josephson of Cardiff for Physics (his Josephson Junction was a vital part in establishing the success of the World Wide Web), Martin Evans of Cardiff University for embryonic cell research, and the philosopher Bertrand Russell for Literature. OK, it may be argued that Russell was not really Welsh, but he was born in Trellech, Monmouthshire, and lived the latter part of his life in Meirionnydd (Meirionethshire).

One could go on and on! I hope, however, that I have written enough to show that for a small nation of some three million people we have a past of which we can be immensely proud. It pays sometimes to look in the rear-view mirror and I believe that if only the people of Wales were more fully aware of our past – our history, our story – it would give us much greater confidence in facing – and building – our future.

Highlights from Welsh History is just one of
a whole range of publications from Y Lolfa.
For a full list of books currently in print, send
now for your free copy of our new full-colour
catalogue. Or simply surf into our website

www.ylolfa.com

for secure on-line ordering.

TALYBONT CEREDIGION CYMRU SY24 5HE
e-mail ylolfa@ylolfa.com
website www.ylolfa.com
phone (01970) 832 304
fax 832 782